"With J. Chester Johnson, objectivity and passion coexist naturally. And language, rather than abstracting experience, breathes a direct connection to our tragedies, pettiness, bones and sweat and exaltation."
— Jean Mellichamp Milliken
The Lyric

"These delightful poems are self-contained, succinct and declarative, admirable for their shapeliness and humor, their aptness and originality."
— John E. Smelcer, poetry editor
Rosebud

"Chester Johnson has crafted these poems — over years and miles — with a precision and economy one might not expect in poems that also *sing* so beautifully. They have a jewel-like spiritual depth: facets and illuminations revealing themselves as one gazes, new ones appearing upon re-reading."
— Barbara Crafton
Episcopal priest and author

"Poet Johnson, author of ten chapbooks, has now published a collection of poems — some old, some new, but all riveting — for those who appreciate the poetic rhythm of our language. The poems are about people, places, and ideas. And readers of the poetry of today will find *St. Paul's Chapel & Selected Shorter Poems* a thoroughly enjoyable read that they can pick up and read again and again."
— Art Bounds, editor
The Pegasus Review

"Reading a poem in J. Chester Johnson's current collection pauses a sensitive reader at its conclusion to re-read the poem and become involved in the poem's experience. That is what an excellent poem does."
— Ray Foreman, editor
Clark Street Review

"The selection of poems was a delight. The verse contains crystalline moments for the reader. Still life or heroic verse, both are equally captivating."
— Ellen Shull, editor
Palo Alto Review

"Gifted. A fine talent for the phrase."
— Allen Tate

"My reaction to (Johnson's) work, wholehearted as it was, did not come near to envisioning the scope and quality, the prodigality of (Johnson's) accelerating career."
— William Stafford

"The collection will please the many people who enjoy twists of language, clever phrases and rhymes, and wily punch lines. Lively, entertaining; and with courage in its lightness."
— Constance Hunting, poet
editor, *The Puckerbrush Review*

"Wherever my gaze fell I read good lines."
— Isaac B. Singer
Nobel Prize Winner for Literature

"Truly a master of the difficult art of compression."
— Albert J. Guerard

"When the staff editors and I at *Hawai'i Pacific Review* decided to publish J. Chester Johnson's poem, 'Fear of Flying,' we were impressed with his ability to bring nature into the scenario of the 9/11 catastrophe with his reference to birds in the first stanza, which was rather unexpected. We were also impressed with his ability to conjure up images of flight and tie them to the unfortunate victims of 9/11 who chose to jump from the building rather than endure the holocaust inside. And amidst all this, a sudden, fleeting fascination with 'A swatch of cellophane (swelling) heavenward, higher still,' followed by the poignant question, 'How does it happen some things/ Rise air-tucked without ties,/Staves, or other fast catch-mes?' Then, the final question that we all fear to ask: 'Flying is good for business, we're told,/But is it good for us?' brings together a fascinatingly composed poem, not unlike many of his others. Johnson's poems demonstrate his very canny ability to turn an unexpected phrase, his wry sense of humor, and his penchant for getting at the heart of problematic situations that we all would do well to ponder."

— Patrice M. Wilson, editor
Hawai'i Pacific Review

"J. Chester Johnson's succinct, direct style is a bracing tonic for those whose sensibilities and sensitivities have been battered by the obfuscations of the modern vernacular. His work is full of spirit, heart, and a sly humor based in delight. Seldom does plain sense seem so uncommon. The reader is better and wiser for the experience. One hopes the wide cultural world will discover and embrace this new found land of enchantment."

— Phil Wagner
ICONOCLAST Magazine

St. Paul's Chapel

&

Selected Shorter Poems

J. Chester Johnson

Introduction by Edward Mendelson

3-6-18

To Rev. Dr. Donald Richmond —

*Your comments about my written
work were so thoughtful and appreciated!
With best wishes from the author —*

Chester

St. Johann Press
Haworth, NJ

ST. JOHANN PRESS

Published in the United States of America
by St. Johann Press
P.O. Box 241
Haworth, NJ 07641
www.stjohannpress.com

Library of Congress Cataloging-in-Publication Data

Johnson, J. Chester
St. Paul's Chapel & selected shorter poems / J. Chester Johnson
p. cm.
ISBN-13: 978-1878282-61-3 (pbk. : acid-free paper)
ISBN-10: 1-878282-61-1 (pbk. : acid-free paper)
I. Saint Paul's Chapel & selected shorter poems II. Title:
St. Paul's Chapel and selected shorter poems. III. Title.

PS3560.O3786S7 2006
811'.54—dc22

2005053189

The paper used in this publication meets the minimum requirements of the American National Standard for Information Sciences—Permanence of Paper for Printed Library Materials, ANSI/NISO Z39/48-1992

Manufactured in the United States of America

Introduction

A volume of selected poems should be a guidebook to three separate landscapes, each with its own complex history and variable climate. The first is the book's purely verbal landscape, a vista of rhetorical peaks and contemplative valleys that extends from the cultivated fields of formal stanzas to the wild forests of free verse. The second is the inner psychological landscape of the poet, shaped by his intellect and passions and by his sense of his own past and future. The third is the social and cultural landscape to which the poet responds, where the prominent landmarks are the political or moral disasters and virtues on which his private vision focuses.

Chester Johnson's selection of his shorter poems is a guidebook of precisely this kind. Among its many and varied satisfactions, its variety of technique and emotion is one of the deepest. These poems range over a wide verbal, intellectual, and emotional territory that includes unsettling moments of darkness—in both the inner and outer worlds—and reassuring evocations of light. But all its elements cohere in a unified vision. In the phrase of the old Baedeker guides, these landscapes are "worth the journey."

The verbal landscape of this book—the form and texture of the poems—is more than enough reason to explore it. From the extravagance of the early "Jupiter" to the late, laconic "Quatrains" and "Haiku," this is the work of a poet for whom poetry is not merely a record of thoughts and feelings, but a way of thinking and feeling itself. One difference between a poet and a versifier is that a poet instinctively thinks about the world in terms of poetic language and through the medium of poetry itself, while a versifier thinks in terms of plain prose and then laboriously translates his thoughts in poems. Shakespeare understood the degree to which he thought in poetry when he wrote in a sonnet: "my nature is subdued/To what it works in, like the dyer's hand."

Chester Johnson makes explicit his own poetic habit of thought in such poems as "Adversative Conjunctions" and "Abduction of the Apostrophe 's' " and what is explicit in these poems is implicit in all his others. His work is governed not so much by an habitual personal style, but by his ability to find for each of his poems a form, style, and diction precisely suited to its subject. As most poets know—but few will say—an insistent characteristic style can help a poet to create a public reputation, but can also narrow his range and hinder his ability to grow and change. "The problem of every man and writer," W. H. Auden wrote, "is at all times essentially the same, namely first to learn to be himself and then to learn to be not himself." The variety of form and language in this book is the means by which Chester Johnson has learned both these things.

For a poet, unlike a versifier, the greatest temptation is to imagine that form and style are all-important, that form and diction matter more than justice and love. But this book is the work of a poet who faces and resists that temptation. The second of the three landscapes in the book—the inner, personal landscape of the poet himself—has the strong, subdued quality of a man in his middle years who has retained his youthful passions for virtue and love, but has no regrets for lost youthful fantasies that seemed to promise perfectibility in himself and the world.

The verbal world of these poems is shaped by their author's style and diction, but the psychological and moral world of the poems is shaped by something deeper: a private grammar of thought, an organizing logic that governs the ethical and intellectual understanding. For Chester Johnson, this grammar of thought is theological. Every event in his poems, no matter how apparently transient or insignificant, is understood in its relation to permanent truths, whether or not those truths are named in the poem. Even his dirty jokes have theological points to make. Chester Johnson's theology is that of the Anglican Communion, that hybrid of Catholicism and Protestantism in which the individual world of the voluntary will and the shared visible world of ritual and the body have equal rights, and the excesses to which each of these worlds is tempted are inevitably set right by the resistance of the other.

The combination of personal experience shaped by a theological grammar helps to make these poems, as a whole, a repository of the kind of wisdom that George Eliot described in *The Mill on the Floss*:

> The middle-aged, who have lived through their strongest emotions, but are yet in the time when memory is still half passionate and not merely contemplative, should surely be a sort of natural priesthood, whom life has disciplined and consecrated to be the refuge and rescue of early stumblers and victims of self-despair.

"It Happened on East Shelton Street" is one of many poems in this book that enact this sort of priesthood, with its understanding of the kind of marriage that is "most entire." In "Evensong," a couple eschews "an outside world. . .for the sake of intimacy," but the book as a whole moves easily between the inner world and the outer one.

The book's third landscape—its outer, public one—is torn by violence and injustice, some of it remembered from the segregated South of the poet's childhood, some of it experienced in the vulnerable New York City of the poet's adulthood. Yet that same landscape is sustained and renewed by quiet acts of courage and endurance, and these poems portray a world beleaguered, realistic, and brave.

The book's title poem, "St. Paul's Chapel," displays in compressed form the virtues of the whole. The poem needs no commentary beyond, perhaps, a brief gesture pointing to the line, "It stood among myths. It stood among ruins." What remains standing when myths fall into ruins is truth, and these poems, like all authentic ones, bear witness to a truth.

Edward Mendelson

Foreword

A few words that introduce almost forty years of short verse should, at the outset, acknowledge the role of geography in the selected poems. Of course, landscapes meta-morphose right under a poet, and the verbal rendering of the unsteady journey across them can hardly be a fixed and fast declaration. That being said, verse, compiled for *St. Paul's Chapel & Selected Shorter Poems*, is a much better map for surveying the close territory than prose would be.

The order of the verse in *St. Paul's Chapel & Selected Shorter Poems* is eclectic and more thematic than chronological. While I haven't been diligent about dating individual poems over the years, a faultless recording was hardly possible, taking into account a sustained revision process. Too, the quatrains and haiku were written here and there (mostly without any expectation of publication) and then stored, often for long periods of time, in cabinets or loose-leaf notebooks; these poems have, therefore, proven by far the hardest to chronicle with any precision.

I began writing verse in high school and continued with it in college, but it wasn't until I reached my early twenties that I started to compose real poems, several of which are included in *St. Paul's Chapel & Selected Shorter Poems*; others illustrate more recent verse. Most poems are revised from their original (often published) versions. The length of an individual piece was the determining factor in the assignment of a poem to the longer (a volume to come later) or the shorter verse collection, but, in addition to sorting by length, my personal like or dislike of a poem became the basis on which a piece of verse was chosen or discarded (and a large quantity did fall to the floor, figuratively speaking). It should also be mentioned that quite a few chapbooks containing a sizeable number of poems included in *St. Paul's Chapel & Selected Shorter Poems* have

had limited circulation, and, as shown on the acknowledgement page, many of the poems in the volume previously appeared in newspapers or literary journals.

This shorter verse has undoubtedly been affected, to some extent, by my work on the Psalms. For the better part of the 1970s, I participated, as a member of a seven-person drafting committee, in the retranslation of *The Psalter*. This retranslation, employed for liturgical and communal services, is now contained in *The Book of Common Prayer* of The Episcopal Church (U.S.A.); later, this version was also adopted for the *Lutheran Book of Worship* and *The Book of Alternative Services* of the Anglican Church of Canada. Admittedly, poetic features of the Psalms bear little resemblance to the style and texture of much verse being written today; nonetheless, when I compose my own poems, I'm sure the special function of the caesura, the personality of the cursus, and the braiding of strophes, as practiced in the Psalms, insert themselves now and then into my verse—without any conscious decision on my part. At the same time, I've utilized common forms, such as terza rima ("Elegy To A Distant Son"), and more modern schemes—one of which, "elastic rhyme" ("Back In The Garden" and "Child of Mercy"), I developed and which I have explained in other writings.

And then there was September 11, 2001, and all that followed. The poem, "St. Paul's Chapel," was originally published in *Episcopal Life* in September, 2002 and, at approximately the same time, went on display as one of twelve exhibits in the Chapel by Ground Zero commemorating the events of a year earlier and honoring the use of St. Paul's Chapel as a relief center for the recovery workers during the eight-month cleanup period at Ground Zero. Since then, copies of the poem have been distributed as a handout, as a memento, for those touring St. Paul's—after more than two years, by the spring of 2005, about two million persons had passed through the Chapel. The poem, which has now appeared in a variety of outlets, is contained in this volume.

At an early age, I received a lot of encouragement from several poets, including William Stafford, Allen Tate and James Dickey, who were supportive without urging conformity for my style to become more consistent with their own. In fact, the influences on my verse have come from sources quite apart from those poets—which

simply goes to show that poets shouldn't need to be emulated to enjoy and value the verse of others.

The arrangement of accents on occasional lines in these short poems may initially resound as slightly unusual for some readers. Southerners—at least those who talk without a broadcaster's insouciant "tongue"—frequently don't accent the same syllables that other speakers do. This factor can differentiate the cadence of some lines written by a Southerner from those written by someone who's a native of, let's say, Akron, Ohio. A Southerner by birth, upbringing and speech, I admit to periodic struggles, traced from effects of "the accent," with the scansion of some poetry. For instance, take a common word like "intent"; most will, as a rule and practice, accent the second syllable every time, but I readily accent the first in a normal flow of conversation. Nonetheless, troublesome speech traits are not unique to Southern poets. For example, W. H. Auden recognized his own related problems with sound recognition when he admitted late in life: "It makes me wince when I see how ready I was to treat *–or* and *–aw* as homophones. It is true that in the Oxonian dialect I speak they are, but that isn't really an adequate excuse." Once a reader gets the hang of it, however, a moderately different access can occur, and I also believe readers have a high degree of tolerance for this sort of thing anyway.

There are several poems (I think they will be obvious—among them, "Jupiter" and "And Cherokee Sundown") I have included in these pages primarily to illustrate an earlier period of writing. A few readers may find them suspect, although others still say the older poems are agreeable—the volume of selected shorter poems wouldn't be representative (nor, I think, credible) without them.

J. C. J.

St. Paul's Chapel

&

Selected Shorter Poems

St. Paul's Chapel

It stood.   Not a window broken.
             Not a stone dislodged.
It stood
when nothing else did.
It stood
when terrorists brought September down.
It stood among myths. It stood among ruins.

To stand was its purpose, long lines prove that.
It stands, and around it now, a shrine
of letters, poems, acrostics,
litter of the heart.
It is the standing people want:
To grieve, serve and tend
celebrate the lasting stone of St. Paul's Chapel.

And deep into its thick breath,
the largest banner fittingly from Oklahoma
climbs heavenward
with hands as stars, hands as stripes, hands as a flag;
and a rescuer reaches for a stuffed toy
to collect a touch; and
George Washington's pew doesn't go unused.
Charity fills a hole or two.

It stood
in place of other sorts.
It stood
when nothing else could.
The great had fallen,
as the brute hardware came down.
It stood.

The Wreck

It took ten years to gather
the nerve to write this poem.
Shades on a mirror
scare timid words away.

It was like this:
Opal was toting groceries home
after an extended trip to Phoenix.
As she crossed Main Street
with an armful of nothing much
(now bear in mind, she was 80 years old
and slight in size, very slight in size),
suddenly out of nowhere,
                    a pickup truck
 (quicker than wind chill)
barreled through the old woman,
spotting her some 40 feet down the street
(before the two, tangled, came to rest).
She whispered to the check-out girl,
who came to tend,
"There isn't a place that doesn't hurt."
Opal passed away
(as many here paraphrase)
of internal injuries six hours later,
released from a resuscitator.
It was like that.

There are some things about which
one can not write
'til the shades fall from reflection,
and passage transforms
her safely to the curb.

How An Athlete Got Over It

Jake was once an athlete,
            demon of the strut, float of a walk;
And flexing for show was a gift from God.
Adam in a natural state.

While the audience forgets and the athlete should,
Jake divined another game, made more cunning,
            distilled into faithless sex.

Women, women, take them all,
For he was, in a muscular sense,
            potent Zorba of the old sweat suit,
            Zeus with a torn cartilage.

The pleasure declines with repetition,
            he groused, but too many were too few
            to exercise for
Tournament champion, a record vault.

Then tough Louise came along –
            javelin thrower and ascetic, world-beater
            and grit-machine –
Who pounded Jake so frail and pale
That he soon forgot Gail and Dale.

The Killer

Pull the trigger, find the shock.
Sun, moon, the meteors – these,
No one to remember a thing.
Sundowns drain into estimates
After a shot's gut-fired
And the target hit at bull's-eye.

That's the way we want it:
One mission, one instrument,
The skill to make it happen.

Even for one who tastes more salty blood
Repeatedly, the routine shall not stale:
Sweat reigns, spit vacates,
          odor washes a moment.
One shot – that's what I'll give myself.
Head straight, no blinking;
Relax the hold, breathe halfway.
I'm ready. Yes.
A figure falls before the recoil evaporates;
As my eyes widen, as I murmur and distill
To this: I steal the strength of these I kill.

Gettysburg Tranquilized

Blue and gray samples, false sabers,
Witness awards: For sale
At the Visitors Center.
It's too comfortable by far.

Spectators at a heroes' blood garden;
Let's try not to imagine,
For the soldiers, once here,
Still can't restrain themselves. . .
After histories, approbation and such.

Take the Wheatfield, for example:
Four thousand men cut down
During five hours of fighting
Over an area no more sweeping
Than three American football fields;
Bodies stacked three deep,
Luring speculation; lured creeds abound.

Then Little Round Top for synoptic views,
And Pickett's Charge to mock a tormented South.

Places and recitals display fragility
Against horror and surrealio that
Happened here: Death beyond death,
Death, death (summoned, caught, rushed, escaped),
Death diminished, death feared and unfeared,
Death undone untinctly (death made too small
Or too relevant by too much).

People who attend today do imagine
But mustn't, for we shouldn't;
Gettysburg tranquilized
Can not be believed.

Lee and Meade hammering it out;
Half head, flecks of flesh, knuckles   live meat
In flight; troops came to collide
And weren't disappointed.
150,000 arrived, one-third minced
With all or parts of their bodies
Slathered over roots and eviscerated season
After three days.

Longstreet and long grass,
Chamberlain, partisan,
Hood and brotherhood,
Warren, amen.

We move on to Cemetery Ridge
For a final face of battle;
A boom box explodes,
Couples munch hot dogs and lore,
Someone hums "Dixie,"
While still others
Have modern games in mind.

We hear a whisper, then harsher thuds,
As soldiers of a blue brigade clamor into ranks
Into the ready grip for conflict:
For a mind to imagine,
I must have a death to give.
For a mind to imagine,
        inhabit a colossus,
               the soldiers' terra incognita.

Another Sultry Moment

Flesh is the thing.

Sere, rough-hewn leather says
We've gotten old and baroque.
Fruit-flavored and spot-free, suppleness
Tells a much different story.

We knew the latter once
When sap rose daily, nightly, continually,
Not deciduously, no seasonal
To seasonal preservation,
No waiting upon a lambent pulse.
Flesh was the thing.

Now sap clogs
On its way, slow to surface
On the parch-high of thinner skin;
And yet we've learned the tricks
Of trading guile for unction
And grit for sauce.
Wizened in a grasp of sentient claims,

Flesh is still the thing.

Irony At The Armchair

Oh, would Lincoln have contracted laryngitis
               traveling to Gettysburg,
Or Socrates could enjoy the cocktail party anyway. . .
As George Wallace, on his deathbed,
               didn't remember his race,
Or as Joyce chose a heroic couplet for a tombstone,
               while Elvis was never, ever sighted. . .
Oh, Bible parts should be banned in the Bible Belt,
               and Einstein was not relative at all. . .

Resting headlong in a slouch,
I swear irony is fantasy under control.

Part Two

Contents

Acknowledgments

Grateful acknowledgment is made to the editors of the following publications in which some of these poems initially appeared, often presented in somewhat different versions:

Anthology 23 (Bay Area Poets Coalition), ArtLife, The Aurorean, The Catbird Seat, Clark Street Review, The Connecticut Poet, Cumberland Poetry Review, Episcopal Life, Evansville Review, Fauquier Poetry Journal, Hawaii Review, Hawaii Pacific Review, Icon, The Iconoclast, International Poetry Review, Journal of New Jersey Poets, The New York Times, Northern Stars Magazine, Palo Alto Review, Parnassus Literary Journal, Pearl, The Pegasus Review, Poetalk, Poetry Forum, Poetry Motel, Poet's Voice, Potpourri, Red Owl, RiverSedge, St. Joseph Messenger, The Lyric, Timber Creek Review, Tucumcari Literary Review, Westview, Westward Quarterly, WoW, Writer's Exchange, Writers' Journal.

Numerous poems in this volume, also often presented in somewhat different versions, were originally included in the author's following chapbooks: *An American Sequence; Oh America; Shorts: On Reaching Forty; Shorts: For Fun, Not For Instruction;* and *Freda's Appetite.*

To Freda,
whose songs and silences
are carried in these verses

Back In The Garden

The serpent has requested of the apple tree:
"Except for unjustified violence and such jazz,
That aside, what will be the greatest sin of all?"
Its branches astir, the apple tree replied:
"Doubtless (as nothing comes close that I foresee) –
Idolatry, idolatry, idolatry.
It'll be everywhere, a crude potpourri:
Work for some, shrine of power for others,
Food, drugs, incandescent sex, proud wine,
Sports and money, enough white marble;
An endless number of things and stuff
Without which (the mystique of it) the children of God
Will think they can not live for a week."
The serpent, replete with smiles, went his own way;
For the game was set and the fix complete.

Night Call

I, for one, need no safe exit
out of the wild universe of the midnight café,
coffee not much instantly,
rain stuck to shoulders of the storm.

I, for one, know my steps away
warn of solitude, as words hushed
are now repeated in mute resonance;
beer mist, lascivious smoke, loss,

Night calls
gather the loose and dangerous strays
the moral day rejects, so it is said,
but I, for one,
belong to the night, for it and I
refuse the traces and lies of daylight,
and we are one.

Poeta Comicus

So you'd be a poet, huh?
What, with wild cloth askew, strange glue for an eye.

Who would write that rubbish
Doesn't have the glide to be one more rock star
      though it may have been tried,
And who would write the tripe
Can hardly fine-tune another dean
      of etiquette any time soon.

Convention will make you pay for going there;
You'll be banished to Bedlam or ne'er-do-where.

But if you must, say it straight for the start
Of things left unsaid – and not for the art.

Lover Denied

What you have heard
       and known and I haven't
I envy,
for it was done
without me in mind.

You say I miss music I never hear?

Love
 – whatever tune
has been unknown for much too long –
ignores its ignorance.

A Love Poem

The earth shook, went bad
     and came 'round again.
We caught an evening sky
     and put all disturbed objects
     and crooked things back together,
And the earth coalesced
     around our love
     and slipped back into a smooth slumber.

At The Bar

Sipping, I hear the wine contend:
"Grapes hold their sweetness in reserve
. . .to hold control."
At the bar,
We also add tips and traps.

Elegy To A Distant Son

I

You will not know by any telling, Son,
The thoughts that I have softly shared with you.
At once, you weren't there (from divorce they run!) –

And separate by place and unlike view,
We cracked apart as though we were the rot.
Myself for us was said to be untrue.

You have your toys, mild talcums, and low spot
Now at the ductile age of twenty-four,
And I have mine, now long in tooth and squat;

We share a little only, nothing more –
While even on our way to fluent ground.
What's done, these coupled traits we're to ignore.

You trekked into another side around,
Another side of scrubs and pits unbound.

II

We should forage by two to bear us best,
But you have gods among brambles and trees,
The gods you chose without my watchful test

Around the deeper bush, as I, by degrees,
Have learned to practice distance to survive.
We quicken sports news, spun as similes,

With pitchers, catchers, scores (as points alive
And hugs), for father-son things were denied
From which a verbal coven could derive.

And now from here? Just simply put aside,
For you'll do yours, and I will go to mine.
Yet deep within the sleep of foster-tide,

And maybe on a day of law or sign,
You will discover something we define.

III

And maybe at the birth of any child
Or moments moiling through the smoke of loss,
Or left behind, a pair of fools, self-styled,

Will shed from us this tumid albatross
Before, again, it madly perseveres.
(What makes our mutual blood a double cross?)

And if the promise, "Welcome back," appears,
We'd squinch badly for lines so meant to save –
A flutter to both tongue and vow adheres

To doubt reprised and restive words, but brave.
A safe distance opens a safe landscape.
While musing on the slights that we forgave,

I stalk your many secrets I'd reshape,
And you're just moving faster to escape.

Bon Appetite!

To know you,
one must know
something about you. . .
You're first generation American,
whose parents fled
Anti-Semitism, given voice
in excuse and its kind. . .
Certainly enough to rally
your appetite
to be broad and less likely,
perpendicular to the storm
so to fight it, and
inimical to naivete,
huge and stable
are the desires you issue
and sophisticated anger,
bon appetite!

At best, historical events
explain mere circumstantial matters,
not what makes you herself,
so that history stops short
of attesting to a native taste
or rapacious appetite
to correspond to life's behavior,
its immortal and liquescent reasons. . .

Devil Said

Dreams err, of course.
They're excessive
and, therefore, must be tempered.

It's simply a law of nature
that the time of promise can't last long for any of us,
as a brute course prevails,
as a procrustean, thick fog covers a beckoned spring.

One becomes what one can –
with a caricature of what could have been,
for we know better than stone
the cost of trying to be more
than one should be.

Clouds

The clouds were poised, and the hair was combed;
the outfit chosen, the subject declared:
Truth would be pursued.
Against the walls of nomenclature
and in the tangled roots of words,
we were ready,
Tongue-tied on incantations we murmured
but couldn't recite.
There were clouds heavy to rive,
lightning at the cusp,
claps so bearable whenever retrieved.
And while we waited for a clarion high,
The impervious clouds simply floated by.

Culture Of Lies

Someone told a secret.
It expanded to many more.

As from small corn
Sprouts the great tale   . . .When we heard

It's a matter of something warm
Exposed too long.

Fable Wood

How the bark
of a cedar tree
sounds so human. . .

Beating the tree trunks
with hollow branches,
I hear
my ancestors   on horseback –
rhythmically hooves
grab at each thud
against eternal wood.
(The faster the beat
the louder the hooves.)
Then silence,
then a hum on molden tongues,
then a chant:
"Return to the forest, where wood
cants a story of the first legend."

Ruination Quite

He's into ruination – and why not?

'Taters rot, warblers fall,
Safety fails, and cycles crest.

So he gathered tumbles and a squall
Around his hutch to work out the wrest.

Afterlaugh

And let one who

    believed there is no God

Tell a half joke

    after he's in the sod

About himself

    who couldn't face the face of the Great Belonger,

About himself –

    an atheist who isn't one any longer.

Genesis

The nature of things
            – water that moves
            – the bread of oxygen
            – such
                      (before the latent loss
                        has taken root and blooms)
is first naïve,
        then harmed.

Crazed

A puddle a fool, one dog philosopher too –
A sparrow, of course, democratic tool –
Or sundown, the eternal no; poems?
An image, hiding a hidden shutdown,
Would hide the gaff and laundered mind.
These silly imagists, too cute by a half.

The Angered

I, now baited and re-baited in the mist
        of occasion, the moment
he saw for revenge.
(Symbols springing everywhere
        to gather madness –
        broken panes, sheared forms, odd music –
And through it all, we effected logic
        to tailor our own kind of anger.)
Yes, he saw for revenge, but
there was no reason,
for I'm no Joshua and he no Og of Bashan.
He seethes and seethes
        with no opportunity waived,
the occasion untextured, untutored. . .
        and he waited and waited
        and ground his teeth smooth
        and gnawed the personal system red
        and faked the meaning of it as well.
Oh if I knew when the hit, increased by suspension,
        would come,
        I'd be damagingly aware. . .

Doppelganger

– reflections at a broken window

I, am, I, and no one else. . .
Surprisingly at an angle.
I'd be someone else, really,

But I'm hampered. . .by in between;
For other toes and joints
Don't match,

Or I become overheated
Or submerged under ice
To wet fog over glass.

I, am, I, and no one else. . .
But I can't smug it out
There worrying away

Between a half I have
And the half to someone else.

Overheard On The Platform
In The 59th Street Subway Station

Making "do" is hardly enough.
To be truly human,
one must build something very tall. . .

                And only those who would
                could know that "do"
                won't do.

Particularly. . .
        in the City
as adept gauges take charge,
as those gadgets and fillers waxing technical (and also deft)
        transform to progress,
to barter, to treasury,
to commerce beyond subtle sales. . .

                And as the excesses of something distinct
                release the excesses of something succinct.

Adversative Conjunctions

Oh a cadence soars along atop mere syllables. . .   we're
                    on an undulating ride with no fret at all of abruption,
And so pleased our utterances are also ringing,
                  "O say can we sing by the dawn's early delight?". . .
An uninterrupted motion rolling, lumbering therapeutically,
        epically, elliptically, euphorically
        will absolutely bump into nothing,
We aspire. . .
And then, and then, ground off our lilting circuit,
            we detect a rising bass version
            of adversative conjunctions,
As "but" turns us around
And "nevertheless" spoils the ride.
                  Now we're back where we began
                  at stasis, still ardent, still abeyant.

". . .the well-known banker was guilty of fraud."

He carried shame,
He lugged it home.
He washed it long,
He washed it through.
The water turned green,
The wife red.

Venus de Milo's Call To Arms

I have been far and wide
And dwelled on a sullen side.
Now I'm not what you'd call mod,
But I'd drop an old stone god
To reach for arms stone denied.

Does One Ever Think In Poetry?

Does one ever think in poetry?
                    Some say Mozart thought only in music,
and Auden in staccato rhythms.
                    Many say devils and angels
fight for the ears of us all,
                    and the battle hymns of the two
reputedly translate into a language of gods. . .
I, for one, believe it,
                    not because poetry is grand,
or music rates as the bravest mode of travel.
                    No, I've now lived long enough
to hold that both good and bad
                    have their places in this world,
and the outcome of the dialectic struggle
                    rushes to become the chorus of divine cries. . .
And all the rest,
all the rest,
merely rehearses the possibility
that we think in poetry. . .

Advanced Degrees

They're too old
    to mock each other
    with nuisant games.

As they play,
    they knowingly
    conspire to play

And acknowledge less
    bears more with age

And prove easily
    aegis of ease.

Devil In My Bowels

Into the wastelands
The devil so expands.
Swish, Pow, Bang, Plunk.
The devil also stunk.

Charlie's Boy and I...

You might as well bite the hand that feeds
You and pick your teeth with wild oats;
For that's how things really are.

They say you can't be wild and pure at once,
But Charlie's boy and I, we beg to differ:
To divide the text roughly doesn't work, ever –

For, according to every way but loose,
You must be wild
About what you'd also be pure.

It

It has fancy feet
and does impossible things.

It seduces best and good alike.

It never compromises;
it works miracles
and can trade
midgets into giants.

It's sticky and sweet;
it makes candy affordable.

Its name is money.

The Desert Monk

(Karnak first, Sinai versed)

*

I was born from mystery into mystery
And, through mystery, I will leave.
In between, I wait. . .

*

When there's nothing,
That's something.
And enough. . .

*

For God does not need to show proof
And thus inquires. As I search,
I linger with God. . .

*

If you find God only by proof,
Then that's an argument
Between you and God. . .

*

And if, by chance, you profess
To understand, you
Haven't tried.

The School On Rue Des Rosiers

Paris, France

(165 enfants juifs de cette
ecole deportes en Allemagne
durant la seconde guerre mondiale
furent extermines dans les
camps nazis.) N'oubliez Pas.

To lament is to warn. . .
No slaughterhouse
of innocence can be explained so.
A cosmic loss
can only be reached
by a cosmic soul. . .

what merciful eye
forgot to look their way?

Sums of laughter
are disguised by honor
and drama tonight;
only a plaque
remains to remind me
children once resided
where echoes now control. . .

what merciful eye
forgot to look their way?

How can crimes and insanity
be so near so many
among balance and delight?
I know and do not know,
for fear of the answer
keeps me timid;

~ 41 ~

so be it, monuments and plaques
to commemorate our failures,
not our successes. . .

This morning,
I hear a baby cry
above Rue des Rosiers,
suggesting once again
I yet turn away
the fortunes and recourses
of loss and the designs
and progress of pain. . .

what merciful eye
forgot to look their way?

The morning light now
rises above
the school on Rue des Rosiers,
and soon, the chatter
of children will again rule a courtyard.
Music will be heard,
and a boy will
not notice one girl
predicts and surveys
her own absence. . .

To lament is to warn. . .
Let those who play here now
know (without despair or numbness)
that great accidents befall great people,
great evil befalls great good,
and the greatest fall
always dances
near the greatest dancer.

Friday Nights On Hyatt Field

Someone kept Hyatt Field in shape
               where we knocked each other around.
The Billies, very district champs,
               and I have the high school scars to prove it.
Flair (or was it just flamboyance?),
               a game (a roar?) by football in public contact. . .
               Down into the grass we would grind our qualms
and mangle the grinding by the other side,
               as pain fell by demand into place.
"Hammer it out a yard at a time,"
               the town prophet decreed by bark
and rolled us home bastards even further:
               "A split lip for first and ten,
a broken nose for six points more.". . .
               We drove on surely to the sacrifice
for a greater good of town and team.
What tempest gods goading this pain do we gratify?
By any name, there's nothing reverential
               gasping at liquid air in an airless meadow
among smells of athletic steam in grassy rows,
               a turf roughed by flesh-flaying cleats.
There's nothing notional or subtle about it
               (not as a work in progress or thin, lithe strokes
below the waist) – not the glare from multi-eyed lights,
               band music in cacophony
and cheers "to keep the lead out,"
               or a full stadium to make it worthwhile.
Even a little blood left on the game can convince us we're heroes.

Ethel's Birthday

She picked up a broad blade knife
(*and conceived*).
Something ignoble brought the abscess too close.

He slept with a drunk's vapor,
Hung leaden on every snore.

Why she didn't know why
Or for how long
The urge had crossed the barrier.
It had, and that was that.

Once she thumbed the blade
        to test the kill,
A hand swept through an instant,
        incising a perfect half-moon
        to link earlobe to earlobe.

We'll drown together, she added;
Blood bubbles for Edgar,
Simple revenge for moi.

Survival Of The Flowers

with deference to William Cullen Bryant

Porky, the elusive brother,
Induced by abundant voices again,
Made it a point to older Jeb:
"We were meant to survive,
Not to lead or nurture.
No matter what Mom said."

They were middle age by then,
And successful
By survival standards.

From death of the flowers
Came a marred message:
So kin leave early, youngest blades
Going first, anything premature.
That's what the family taught:
Don't expect the unexpected,
For it never is.

"We'll change the heading
And split the difference, that's all,"
Tendered Jeb;
A petal dances to a zephyr;
A brothers' floret blooms
In a filament of being.

Stevens' Season

They say Wallace Stevens
    composed verse
      as he counted his way to work;
Steps levitating to a proud ear
    rhythmic pronunciations;
Clarity of verse combined
    with diversions of the street
(And much was lost or much was gained),
    as momentary lapses of metaphor
Brought the business and busyness
    of bustle and brattle
Too close,
Hid a paean for the raised season.

Ich Bin Ein Jude

The wind blows tentative and hot,
dry over unkempt graves in the Jewish section
       of Vienna's Zentralfriedhof.

Weeds claim Jewish headstones,
while Christian ones lie neat and line-tailored
among quiescent ruins; no Jewish families
remain in Vienna to tend the Jewish dead,
       for prejudice extends,
even beyond the democracy of extinction.

The grass shouts, trees wail,
hailstorms upend the fortunes
       of Zentralfriedhof. . .for
once and now Christian,
ich bin ein jude.

Ballad Of The Legends

So came another folk-wise cant:
"Children just don't mix well with Aunt Martha.". . .
What, with manners and butt at odds, purple noise and ivory pose
Dangle in unsuspended rent, in manic-play with two ceremonies

Of uncompromising spit. Not surprisingly, child-bearing
Romps bury tricks and multi-syllabic codes, as small,
But manifold hands can't find a right place, or any place –

While her dry-reft voice, rattling in tin-quake size
And peevish mock, circles toward the nemesis through well-ordered traps.
"Nobody likes your kind anyway,"
Each roars at the other in rival decibels and keys;
Among enemies, how can there be a foreign language?

All're untamed and cantankerous from sum-rough rules of engagement,
Hectoring in their own pesky beat that the litany
Of civil minds does not forgive this or that or primitive rush
Or antique pride either. Is it a matter of bullying –

Youth over age, age against popularity? She simplifies them
(Children of the hubbub) to judge the weight of pure water and the
Primordial curve of speed. "Aunt Martha always cursed speed.". . .

A Pied Through Arkansas

You were meant to travel
From pillar to post to find yourself.
But the road has its own mind;
You can't tell it where to go.
You arrange tales, just tales.

A road also prompts
Odd friends along the trek,
Messengers soon fabled
(Wielding magic
        to tease or persuade);
To feel the heat is
        to know the ploy.

Traveling isn't easy, of course –
Roads often get you only halfway there
Or not at all.
The rest is somehow elusive –
Your manner of describing a map
Confirms a clue, and
Your attempt to have speed pleasing
Sends yet another.
But for a short way around,
The place you plan to land
(Is it Rome or home?)
Can make a road obey.

Evensong

We are by absence joined. . .
Our latent reports and private conventions
assay a strangeness in an outside world
we eschew for the sake of intimacy. . .

Your unwashed stages
stand ever nearer my interior world
and speak wanderingly of it with persuasion,
an hegemony of access this lambent,
this eager to mold a conscious event. . .

We also linger over revelatory things,
no more than two at a time,
not at slight tokens or charming curves
to make things preliminarily better;
no, love begins with one strike
(and maybe another)
at the heart of things,
and then we savor that which we can't change,
those reasons to remain
not casually gazing again. . .
We collect the inference
and curl up, leg inside of leg,
to render an essential part
of the sumptuous preparation. . .

The Lesson

A world spins on its axis. Do you know why? To

teach us a lesson about constancy of notion constantly

at wheel –

        a lesson about lark and laws

           revolving conjoined in constant torque.

Cyclists

Once upon a time, day fell upon night, a mask,
fused upon a death face as the dead at funerals
are meant to come alive.

New territory, volumes of new commentary were
at hand, for we had corrected malevolent angles
with a resurgence of novel facts,

Engaging new lowlands, new threats alive at the margin,
where they begin and solicit as all concede they must
and frame for us again wrecks and wreckage. . .

Immigrant Pause

It was the night before yesterday,
                    And there was no work
For those who would work.
                    It was a lot of work
Getting back to work.

The night of suspicion waited
                    For immigrants working
To work – nativists at the throat,
                    Stink on the sweat,
Emptiness sitting shotgun.

To stare ahead at the search,
                    Which would be all
An immigrant had – to search
                    To find the search.
This was the work there could be.

And those who don't work
                    Still must, for all is work.
It was the night before yesterday,
                    And there was no work
For those who would work.

The Marriage

Now we reach the point

of commitment,   a stone on the ground,

          niche in the history of our condition,

a word across centuries of casual disavowal;

we do exist   and choose. . .

A marriage day comes for everyone, conjugation of

      a propelling and allegoric nexus,

       one throw across a precipice

        (code for past failures);

after a hostile assault on ideals we have maintained
has fallen in turn limp and stale, our loss now unretained.

Marriage lays a line across lines partite;
perhaps, without amendment in sight. . .

Abduction Of The Apostrophe "s"

They thought they were smart,
stealing another state to govern.

Before the crime,
it possessed everything in its path
          and over the verdant horizon,
but then along came tinkers and friends,
          and, voila, the " 's " began
          to be a plural-maker too.

For reasons without a clue, it no longer was enough being
owner of those fecund nouns pounding afterwards.

Surely, whoever coined the "con" that an " 's " should convey so many
          ought to be burned at the stake:
          A few more Cranmers to illume an Oxford square.

I wish I could also break spell-windings,
          mishaps by misplaced letters,
          and remind an editor or two
          of the multiple thefts committed
          on an innocent alphabet.

But this is much worse,
for we're killing off by caprice quiet tools
          that kept the peace.

In The Style Of The Very Earnest Poet

(once pulitzered, twice prized)

If you're looking for the earnest poet
During the night, I can be found in bed
      sleeping it off.

It doesn't matter what I say
      as long as its (with no contractions!) plangent songs
      are a series of over-the-head shots, please –
Aha! Terra-cotta cambers with Mars to induce
      peculiarity, marginalia for allure of difficulty
      (O victory!), as
Oh let the line go off somewhere,
      and it'll find its own liminal and nearly provocative way. . .

Hardly a voice doesn't have
      its own plan for syllables to stream
         away from the poet
Around a corner into puddles,
      immobile and languid,
      to breed trebled marshes into honored discontent. . .

There's simply no apologia, for "poetry makes
      nothing happen," so said a great poet – round, sweet
Words, apricots and a peach bleached hoar,
      semper fidelis upon a blanched garden.

Oh forget rules, lie low
         and take cold temperatures for bathos
Before the next would-be stanza – of
         stridulations coming intoned
To the earnest poet,
         and my poem doesn't have weight, and it shouldn't make sense;
         it is, and that's much better than any old ho-hum.

So he begged for fine arts
         through an exaggerated beard
                  with the mouth wide open.

Eyeing A Frisky Muse

Poems, even small ones, use lots of calories when written well.
Now some think brainpower and intellectual jaunts alone
Place those odd little lines together.

But the body, animated by dactyls and "te-tum, te-tum,"
Exhausts itself, even from mere paeons or anapests;
Whether by ode, Byzantium, or love of limestone,
Poems take the best of us.

And don't count on speed to help, though some will say so,
For speed deludes and suggests magic it can't deliver,
While still others say to be clever
Is to be lyric, if not heroic.

But I say that zing and zest
And energy in the chest
Bring forth the eye that works the page
To craft the lines to tame the rage.

Whirling Toward Hosannas

Billy, the physicist,
thought in wholes, an unending wave,
perpetual dots, parabola true.
Curves make all things possible
as he dropped
into an epicenter,
                    inveterate favorite,
   possibility
for the possibility of love –
Yes, of possible love. . .
      Why it exists
      How it exists   matter not so much,
That it exists will do.

Straight lines terminate and snap.
So one shall not challenge the curve,
    which doesn't stop, ever. . .
possibilities come and stay awhile,
which sets one possibility to be even more possible,
As that very one, however, so very failed
makes the current one
more possible. . .
      Billy had begun,
      and he'll possibly be
      at the place at the time.

All-American

All through the night,
               they all affirm,
all night long murmuring
               about a time when it was always
so easy to manage everything all right.
               One asks another, "Doesn't it also mean
we must now use only all-stars
               all the time?
It's almost peculiar
               the way all around us
and all over, it's all the same –
               whether we're working all out or just waiting,
as we are, all the night through,
               we hear it altogether.
I have wished all along,
               some days all day,
the practice would all clear up,
               and it could be stopped once and for all."

~

Must one be Serbic to be acerbic,
Or Hungarian to be vulgarian?
No, but one must be from Chicago
To be found in flagrante delicto.

Reunited In Café Divino

A word or two about clues in shadows
Tells the story of a family that left home.
It begins with a half-hewn hamlet,
Where silence intones more silence
Amid perspiring, languid breezes
In fern-cornered Monticello,
Where space affirms solitude there;
Slits alive in the rough-edged pine
Vent white vapors off a blinkless sun.
Long roles edit short subjects there.

I once wrote, "If too many generations live
    on the same land, no doubt –
Then the soul of the family
    will finally wear out."
That seems the case; for here we are,
Remnants of an Arkansas aggregation in place,
Taking aggravation and time out,
Taking pleasure in synoptic union,
Into many and healthy appetites
Of Café Divino in New York City.

Friends, compeers, paramours and more,
Who joined the journey, now safely in exile,
Celebrate today with descendents,
Some old, some not, who migrate anew
With those who come from nearby places,
Others of sorts with variegated names.

So can one generation foretell another?
Early traits and behavior attach automatically,
As naturally as chances dissolve along the way,
Whether you wish for the run or not.
But you'll soon render disquieting faux pas
We older-mold types routinely commit;
We, who illustrate failing normal functions,
Revise, recede, reminisce about bad turned best,
Collect useless things and that or also this,
Repeat stories without listeners,
Mumble, mutter, interject, forget birthdays
Or get them wrong or about whom,
And then to fret at lower speeds,
We buy home products in bulk.

'Though chicanery and being rare
Humor some of you seeking a legend,
What do the young really learn from those seasoned
About voluble kinds and reluctant passage? It is said,
Even among slightly wise observers, that the old
Tell tales, sing songs, don costumes and wizened opinions
Merely so the young bear witness to everything
They haven't yet experienced.

At the end, as odd as it may sound, according
To my accounts, the young simply couldn't care less,
Nor should they, if blood has gotten thin
As the family thins out in the urban flood,
With members drawn to distant covens and clamors,
And even if there were romance for the old
In remembering a long-lost Eden to warm the dawn.

From random publicity and its latest rush,
So wealthy in height and handsome too
(And while I'm at risk of sounding preachy just now),
Take this bit of advice for what it's worth:
Acclaim won't be what you do for yourself,
But regrettably will be what others do,
Without sympathy, to you.

And finally, remember, for your own sake and rainbows,
That it's easier for us to instill real family credos
If, whenever in doubt about the way the wind blows,
You pay little heed where the rest of the family goes.

Radicals

It's OK,
If not laude,
To infect
To disinfect.

Intumesce
A thin process
By pretext
To context.

With work to suggest
And work to protest,
From side to side,
A narrow ride,

As reformers shift into an extreme
To elaborate toward another theme –
Coursing through the next triumphant mist
To assemble where counting doesn't exist.

Messenger

Someone, anyone, you,
Do something
        to turn this rite unwound,
Something withheld so long
        has its caption to be
Once and surely forgotten in blind phrase
        or a cold wake of delay. . .

But please make it not so tragic
        that to show me a hero
        is to show me tragedy. . .
Let's find
        a choice for spring:
        Someone who took a chance to run
        to impress upon the rest
That to run, you would first
        defy demigods and
        dance with demons and dervishes. . .

Do something,
Do something
        to let us know
You will miss loss of motion
        more than loss of law. . .

Shortcomings

This will be short
because I don't have much time;
maybe it's an art
the way I can get off the dime.

So here it is:
I become what you want most near
once I put it in forward gear.

Anna and Jack

There was once a girl named Anna,
Who hankered for a banana.
It was hardly a thought to flatter
When she said that size did matter,
As she fell for a horse from Montana.

There was once a bad boy named Jack,
Who gave a girl's bottom a smack.
She turned in a huff and a puff
And cried, "So you want to play rough?" –
As she slipped on spurs for a ride bareback.

Dialing 666

Meet the holy,
She says,
Meaning herself,
Admitting nothing.

You see, she believes
In order
Not to believe,
For the obverse.

Meet the unholy,
You'll observe
The mark of sin,
Clear as through glass,

She breathes to friends
And, bemoaning loss of time,
Then whiles away
Lunch and choices.

Crafty, oblique,
Liberal to an extreme,
She lauds money
To those constrained –

While still stalking a path
To high wealth
Without regard
To Normal Loss.

Money, she deems
In private,
Is the agent
Of love and tidings.

'Cept for those who share
The common heist,
Folks come and go
With a mere pause.

So wallow in defeat
To add excuse,
The best bet
To a clear conscience,

She proffers
To make a point
And, of course,
To hide Gross Intent.

During the day,
She frames and frets;
At night, reminds
Herself of a pact.

So much time spent
At it didn't help,
Talk of self-knowledge
Led to less;

She appeals to those
Most Secure
In code or by notice,
Who sip her compliments.

Others saw a strange shine,
Heard phrases soughing,
Sensed her joy
At Negative Precepts –

Children of her womb
Guess right:
She steals
Much from Beelzebub.

All a Pleasure to
One who depends
On weakness
To feed the stray,

Also relives
The pathological
Urge serving old lessons,
Arming old circles.

We have witnessed
Awful acts
Much too much
In this Age of Fantasy,

But few so often
As telltale moments
In mid-night décor,
Unluckily observed,

She was avowed
To utter pretense,
Fitfully muttering
Mantras distilled.

Though not fashionable
Nor timely
To broach (but
Nonetheless valid),

Agents of a demon
Do dwell among us –
Not so well hidden
Nor aptly tagged.

The cute, the suave,
High tech of today
Control the pace,
So they think,

Demean the prospects
Of evil
In favor
Of the value of the possible,

Then demur to confirm
A script,
Owned and in debt
By sophistry laid,

So made to induce
A cryptic spell
Through nonchalance
Or dispatch to a dark impulse.

It Happened On East Shelton Street

The Smythes,
     Oscar and Leah
        (old brands, to be sure),
fiftyish and folkish,
     freeish in a local sort of way,
        twined of thoughts, body, food,
by vernacular too. . .

No, they're not Winnie and Clemmy,
Nor Cleopatra and Caesar,
No Liz and Richard,
certainly not Romeo and Juliet. . .

As each union
     relies on its own speciality. . .
        as the Smythes bear something
           vitreous, something silted, colloquial, a more
              suffusing favor. . .

This mid-life, yes,
     stuff of which instructive stories,
        less bristled morals are molded,
has taken the grip back from early excess,
     added a mark of effect,
        an equal amount of factual knowledge and easy feast,
and, of course, wistfully learned,
     that later serving of context,
        and it's all very supple,
forgiving, and, at times, most entire. . .

Easter

So here we are, ascending a day no less to first air,
birth from transitional birth, irreducible from non-casual agency,
as generations flee back to this first day of resolution
to learn once more a year how to resurrect
from the mundane, trivial and punishingly lax;
for this – our first Easter together, this your first Easter ever –
act of reconstruction occurs as we invoke this air, unalloyed air,
to seek that which we have sought right along.

Today, a wound liturgized, purposeful collection,
movements destined by practice, abundant rite (summarizing)
shares more to search, to lend something accordant
to lose less instead, and also to pursue a Great Question
with its blind spots, stop signs but curative state,
of which we and our many contrasts are mysteriously a part.

Cliché and irrelevance insurrected and contravened
by healthy divides and circles that most nearly, completely
undo a very temporary and rough-loosed ordeal;
and we finely touch to make certain we're here,
in case, of course, an accident has betrayed
that which we intend or that which we engage (forging
a heightened brocade to keep us sane and resolute);
here we can fall from moment to moment,
capable of surely recalling we'll rise once more.

While the sun greets your face
with spring's low prayer and whisper,
we remember one would not wait again
in a din of cold spirits and ploy.

As we assume the day, I wonder whether, to you,
I've succumbed, a brutist, to delusion, heavy in reverence and custom,
singing psalms, more hymns, and reciting words turning magic
that send a frantic cue to the Great Question,
further along prospective territory
on a road I've found will add to conscious travel.

The endless sleep that's feared by many
weighs long on those who seem to have answers
and suppose it is the rare set of mere tricks, masterfully played,
that save a handful who will be excused. I do not believe it;
for it's not a matter of fast brains or cute quips.
Crude games are for crude children, but that which is difficult
can be handled only by those who can handle difficult things.

You inspire prospects and discern encounters,
yet I find you uncomfortable, while delighted, this day
of birth inside rebirth, reason beyond possible reason,
Easter, venue of the unanswerability of why
we choose to be beyond what we understand.

She

Breathing a sentiment
across an unfashioned room,
she utters bravely
that she's still so trite about these things,
that "a" plus "b" always
equals "c," not even "c" plus. . .
To know is to know
absolute truth is frequently
only half true, so that
facts about us mold
merely half of who we are. . .

That she escaped annulment of unborns
as those before her chose
to let her be, from Europe,
from historically imperious Europe,
where Jews (she still is)
were marked and holocausted,
who were anciently preferred
at the start of the start. . .

That some saw from afar or at hand
and declaimed and decayed
to stay with iconic death,
for there are those who solicit
a romance with black moons
or contend that dying is a guest
explaining broken glass. . .

That she, with ample reasons
to suppose a ritual by *kristallnacht*,
went with others another way
turning, again and again,
    wrest into rest
    and egress into access.

Annie Oakley At Her Blazing Keyboard

She wants to write
And arrive at the next place
With something she'd missed:
Maybe a trace of absurdity near comedy;
Or incarnation's rub;
Maybe a fleshy, azure rock
Nude in a torn pocket;
Or a triumphant Friday
Heading toward a resplendent Sunday
That was, once upon a time,
Brackish-gray and simply palsied.
A magician could she be?. . .
Who can create
Handfuls of beauty or beauties
Lapping over the sides
Of a devil's nest;
Handfuls of lightning bugs,
Winged wasps; or
Membrane clouds (subtle drugs) placed
On the odd corners and shapes
Of stories sneaking out
Among us. . .

She wants to write
With her eyes barely closed
To an epithet,
Not quite seen yet;
While she's riding on the curve
Of a recessive vowel
And on the ellipse of a vagrant,
But heady consonant.

She wants to write
Disgusting palaver and hyperbolic quips,
All the while
Seduced by
The erotica of a footnote.

She wants to write
With thunderbolts from an eagle's claw –
Diving for a phrase
(We've never gotten
Quite right),
Even for the myth of praise.

She wants to write
And know the circumstance
Between happenstance
And something much else. . .

Calling Wolves
In A Language Of Dread

from the vein of Habakkuk

Out of ancient hunger,
A hero wails a pitiless cry,
Made more fierce by bestial noise of technology
Coalescing about these modern hordes.
Content can't match style anymore,
Not as the god of swank has finally seduced
The goddess of probity, who, together, now
Sow delicious sons and daughters
And usher in an epoch of heroes –
Heroes, actors in stealth bearing an immortal image,
Once smiling, anxiously leave a smile, an icon, in turn.
The hunger, heart of the adaptable beast, survives,
Even a full feeding of inexhaustible gluttony.
Spiritus Mundi casually in wait,
While all about, rough skills dominate.

There's no quick context.
Codes break, decency succumbs;
Discourse turns mean with a route around the corner –
Indirect in its simplicity.
Crude messages for masses protect mountebanks and partisans;
When extruding no likeness for its real purpose,
When gathering a faux style
To pretend a true soul
Dwells a hero amid the media –
The media, bound to sound and sight by Magnum Mysterium,
Persuades less and more alike of the peculiar, opening law
That desire for adoration must be the desire for power,
Also awards in public, at some regular whim,
A personality one could not possibly claim,
Plays the role of the All-Present in design:
Omniscient, absolute and divine.

Curious Ways

Grit and wit,
More unalike than opposite;
For I see a dumb one willfully withstand fear
But witness genius escape, charging to the rear.
All of which warns:

> *Expect less from smarts*
> *Than legend imparts.*

Van Gogh's Brushes

For that expression posed,
More valued art supposed,
We now ply color flabby thick and rife
For the way more gaps closed
And, maddened, extend to a still life.

And Cherokee Sundown

And Cherokee Sundown
    will wait out finally
        a dust-charred
           wind-hollowed   scout –

to divination:

I'll be spotted bass
and moon,
the crow and all of rain.
Sands will cover my blood.
I'll be howl
       and desert night.
The sand will color me with moon,
and I'll be the dew that's still in the fist.
I will be the touch
       and a windfall.
Veins will untie me:
I travel a short distance only.

Oh the heavens speak out,
Oh to scatter myself.
The river is no longer wide,
how I cross it in a day
       over the sons I've borne
and wives who stay,
you who carry my youth.

The sun that's with the crow
     knows me,   my name and my cause,
and hangs my distance on this hollow night
       to the stars,
and the dust will catch me in the hills.

                Me,   this life,
I spin this life around me a vein,
and the vein's webbing holds me together.

                Oh I'll be
leaves tear into the wind!
                I am
too full of love I haven't time to free.
        The veins do wear out
this webbing that holds me only to this day.
I'll require you,   my sons,
                        my widows   to my trail,
the sun will shade you more.
Do not lie
            silent into love.
                            Be strong.
                            Speak loudly.
No longer silent
into the shallow moon
                        to the last wind's
whistle and whining
days below the sky,
I hang my strength on the full moon
        on the path to the stars.
I catch the sky in the mountains,
and there the sun's very kind to old fighters –
                sands will not ride me down,
I'm following *The Cherokee Trail of Tears.*

I've seen my past myself once over again now,
I'm not much wiser.
You who come to me through the dust
        and sun yourselves on my light and songs,
follow the water and drink with an open fist,
            drink and swell smoothly,
                                Child of the last hunt,
                                Child of the pace. . .

That this calm,
I bless the days are past the feuds they made
Cherokee Sundown (youth dares me to meaning in the desert)
when days would feud with days
in the heroics of sundown.

Oh to shed myself
    and fall from the hills with an echo
        and sun with the sun
and drink of myself as water,
a desert
    and spring,
first water in coming spring,
    ride with brush and sageweed
and the scattered corn and dry seed.

~

The face of a nation. . .

So it could have been for Dante's Beatrice,

loved but unloving those
who do not swoon
to her beauty.

Edge

Who cares to talk? for we are now at war. . .
The kind with loss of human parts and other friends.
More seraphs (who are they?) have disappeared,
More mutterings hid, and God is worried,
As war hasn't a limit anywhere –
Just turn your head, brushfires now eat forests.
Whatever happened to mere war of words? –
With Ptolemaic pride to aim a phrase;
From armor to adverbs, gerunds as gas masks;
Put slang between blitz and krieg instead. . .
But to bring a cease-fire, the comma's
Weapon of mass construction is its pause.

Jupiter

These universes have learned too little of me already now,
 I stop.
These universes have learned too little of me already now;
      A great motion still goes
   as we've taken on a herd's
      name, someone else's nose,
   another race of words. . .
I try to spell,
     but letters slowly part;
IN this one universe
     we wait to start -
  MATTER outlined by space and duration
       EXploding these universes
    those universes   the ones we are to be,
   so going I have
     we have
     we will
     we have been the imperfect right. . .
And I am logical by far
as I can not know,
and that much more   I'm that much more me
in this one universe
     Things and Answers. . .

Through Projectored light

microcosms   of boundless Gas and germ   to Final Psyche

crossfire_____To Finity

intra-rays condense

& colorless discs

lengthened to a Circle

ellipse toward Infinity.

by the chemistry of cosmos

Giants move in narrow patterns. . .

fumes Oxidize

green gas atmosphered   a luxurious Spray

of Reflectors in frontiers and nitrate. . .

Darling I've got a fast rigor

and it's spilling over you -

we've got a rigor that performs

ice wet sweat over World News.

this stuff we're made of all

these Things and Answers: small,

warm Things you answer which

with things you don't have, rich,

grand answers we undo

with answers worked out too -

only in words!   And stuff

that's not me I constantly bluff.

Just as I like friends

I enjoy consistency

      – I don't understand it all, and that's good;

I like soft sites

I feel warm guides

      – just simple things which touch among the deadwood;

I don't like pain

I worry   for my brother

is my only brother,

and I must wait

for his death-o-gram

      – I have known something called love

                 which was misunderstood;

I feel things,

and some-things in me expand them.

      Ghosts once out of Shells

          under the black arc

    Berserk in Universes and in stars!

They are berserk these lines I draw,

     these lines I draw parallel and long

adjacent to the sane curve (I can not reach center,

     for I deflect off the force of the spin). . .

          Supernature!   frees The Abstract,

        and great forms are loose   Dissolving

my Working line: Why do hollow

men serve their loneliness and old,

worn mothers shame at dryness tense

in their bland and sacred nipples, & then

a father's last wish is his son's

courage, & a parents' message

has a daughter's hate, & still guilty

the rapist reaches for sin when

again jerking warmth from a submissive street?

    – impress   to Disorder   a SCENE -

      No-direction from One Conscious Ablution!

why love

    how to love

       why know one even tender

why

   by counting backwards

        lovers will survive

   by moments backward. . .

a planet advancing   must leave its own

  lovers to howl for cold blood's repair:

   pregnant gains creating size are choked with child, old

    loss moves   undescribed to correction

      begins an entirely new syllable!

And slipping from cracked substance   How answers

 erode with dirt & high pain & slight smiles divide

   chemically – This Universe grew

out of the sad side of each of us,

What Answers!   Sides of each of us, reminders of rock and legend;

These Universes!

Currents   dispersing

exposing Energy. . .

coming up with water to our mouth's wish

loosing   Words –   reflex

fumes of reflex   lost gas fragmenting space

to molecular confusion. . .

Brave nerves and erupting, arrayed

organs rise up in tide to chaotic

Radiations, and black certitude rolls renewed

out of great Combustions of boiled wind,

Mass and Disengaged Bodies,   slight contours. . .

Some part of me still once something

always, this contemporary

Myself (a little space

and its sure sanity) –

who's been Sane in This World?

I've been Sane in This World!!

and this reason is One

of my reasons do not have to be reasons at all. . .

There's probably another world just

before

and another just after This One,

of shape   of solids   nucleus

isolate prevailing Blank Space –   revelations were

new planets blinking in absence;   and I am

some things through and out

                              and were to become

Through these universes and through

I can be alone again or together

with things

                    – an interval stuffed with warm matter

has hardened into that last piece of pure

universe that is totally diverse,

contemporary me. . .And Traveling Through,

A poet in This World may have

been a spy in the Last

and will be a politician

in the Next One.

I disappear   we break   unsocketed

shatter   decomposing   it was

liquified   All was now pledged

and running over, so I spread over, laughed

and rolled (light Separated the disturbance

from unsympathetic length!). . .through Lights and shades

we wandered through uprisings of light and flocks of rain

and heaviness –   chunks fired into unexplored wombs

and gas. . .

                    Explosions!

                    Explosions further!

                                  Explosions join

in larger distance!   Boulders do not miss

me by an inch,   I am influence and carbon,

green gas collects for my fruitful

and swollen chest,   baptismal stumps cleansed

condensing   sunk under me   flip forward

distended   thrive and deflate   then merge

to fill an opening   chip up space! . . .

And Let there be incessant growth,

pounds multiplied to finality;

let electrons meet protons' oath

and calcium its bone, only

measure & counter-measure;   Wait

and let REactions Create. . .

moss weaves rock and wood   into Whole –

legs that began at a stub   pry

    more extended   along a proved edifice –

        arms attach with the cohesion

                of an atmospheric germ!   Accidently

flesh peels on   fingers fasten true –

noses pug up with the well-meant

contraction of cells –   Reassured

spit   grit   veins all adjust in pairs –

enzymes connect –

                              a letter

                                        then words

             all open;   answers build up their

                                        logic chemically –

                                                  while Infirm

Fusions detonate weak composition at conjunctions! . . .

Through uneven obscurity   and a splash

in the streaking fair of sparks, such

that we travel far just to whiff

Once more,   human odors prevail

over the visual display

of flash and ancient cold's dominion!

For I am some things through and out

            and were to become: June and cool

summer were wettest with devout

            sunrise and surprise, molecule

of achievement,   perfect face;

            no winter or 12 months too slow

or hollow by vacant bodies' chase,

            or made witless by a tableau

that memory loves to seize for signs!

            How great colors are that have not

been textures for synthetic shrines;

            This World we've barely seen – what

new WORLDS REAPPEAR!! Blunt and sound,

            more dramatic territories,

these badlands shock, also expound,

        as once more raised, a place agrees

to stay a place; thick locusts blend

        with open fields   a valley sweeps

to a river, and dust must contend

        with cities where a killer weeps

and goes into a Wall to dream

        the arid consequences of amoral seasons. . .

Oh how the mixtures of growing things seem

        to generate warts, crooked wheat and simpletons. . .

   do little for answers!

                because answers can often do next

to nothing

       though they build up chemically. . .

Where there must be more

             much more   and more

    answers;   they're Organic: answers demean

but suffice hope –

        answers decisive made

remiss –

     driven

        substantial

          definitive

             absolute –

answers close,

the answer that is closest,

the best possible

answer that just happens to be the last one

I had today –

the answer erect

crumbles ungracefully;

OH Catharsis retouches all occasional standards

as we allow that suspect forms create,   that an answer suspect

decides me because I'm suspect –

answer

not so suspicious as hope should be

the answer decides me;

but then afterwards

I resound in circumstances and spiel

– I Am at least What I say I Am

I Take on Too Much!

I fail.

So At All After my reasons aren't my

reasons   no reasons   and all the reasons which

made the famous reasons I made them. . .(I've

seen that talking on is just plain talking).

answers I prepare for a superior voice who'd in turn

answer why I'm flat to streets but how

tender to someone who can't occupy a preference;

One more Urge stirs,

is obscured in movement more endowed

and circumscribed INTO indirection more. . .

how we go about measuring our subtle ability

by elemental trust

                shy discipline

                   abnormal promise

      normal plans

                   enviable personal control

(gain or pain?);   What Orgasmic Results (that

extreme eloquence so insistently

apparent to those who recognize

the sounds of their own timid voice)

                             occur now at this clean

place of suggestion

                 have answered us too honestly!

            Oh I

unhesitantly long for an answer too free   answers too chaste

or too vacant then of me in this one

question of where I've been here too long too strange

in this One universe,

                 WORLDS REAPPEAR!!

    whose worlds reappear without my choice

       universally mine of where

I've been in them,

            back in solids

              out in this space

                        switch on time

        too full of presence. . .

ways I held

doctrine in my mouth!

                    Please, you,

with qualities which I love for a lover's sake,

Be like me: which hand

you use to tilt a speech,   huge moment

of a swallow,   bent lust (adjectival occupant

of your throat),   brisk oxygen in your muscle,

and answers at your mouth –

                        Anything you don't

have is my open weakness!   And Be just

like me: ample strength from old bone   small bone

in old skin and the work of a decided jaw;

Be like me: until the likeness reaches

me   reduces me and I hide my dissatisfactions

in your irrepressible difference. . .

answers I made are important

Only in this One Solid,

                        maybe in the Last One

– objects weren't so predominant

– people didn't run into each other's unselected past

– maybe an action had no apparent conclusion

– maybe all absences were tender paragons.

I get accustomed

                and I do hate,

I'm exposed

so I also do learn;

yet my systems can't CONTROL their Ghosts!   for

an inexact and intimidating trace remains of the chemistry

composed from lengthy personal research. . .

And I tell those who participate

to Be Still   a touch does wait for you, and yes,

if you get bored   I'm glad to take the chance

to rouse, as I depend on implicit and unexpected effects;

I speculate

and presage your next spectral epigram

before close explosions set loose

grand Wholes   shall explode us further en route. . .

Always to the asking

when we have to die,

continue to re-sing

miniature, we try

not to ask why we need

to live or to proceed.

By destruction comes the next creation;

brave ellipse   whipping its wise portions dry -

fossils spin away;   I swell while I am young

draining dust spray patterns –   cohesions find

that depths divide;   we're oxidizing with noise

(Explosions further!), Plutonium way

238 to more perfect love;   adroit

Valves tame Rip Open hair streaming,   exhaled

marrow and tissue interrupt your circumference,

Shoot Off!!   molten into one more advanced

lover!

Tongues quite sizzle across assent!

All Speed Vanishing to that nth and rare

Hemisphere!   Truly I'll hold you shot up in debris

from the next Reactor. . .   Mountains split up

to river and slide to flood   float to drop

through the emptied fumous moon;   heads rush,

release to follow subterranean tides;

waters burst loose across false gravity

toward stars;

and an ear shall flow,

brain cells dripping drunk,

ovaries dipped in fumes   disperse   compete –

As fresh flowers sap an eye. . .

love goes down

with a trembling swallow comes up once more

in another long hair!

Planets exhort themselves

into a Liquid mood   their sparks and light coax

correction further;   and when black arcs constrain

heavy contrasts   separate by night's dive –

meteors light us a moment to chase,

attitude to demonstrate, an archetype. . .

Let completion lull always completely
poised on your unfulfilled physique
that finds its resting place
in fulfilled exhaustion. . .
Once you're here speaking deliverance
we find in physical life spring
that continually reforms to again
continually refine.   Shall
an image rise only as formidable
as its perceptible display? . . .Or if aspect and shape abate,
great blinds decline, silhouette lines
at a shoulder contract, writhe and divine?
Oh how Matter REforms floating back another
outcome, as our personal forms come back, bloat,
change and ask why they were favored but spared
little. . .while Answers serve a whimsical way -
even that one lover is in fact really
led by two, when the next event and another
universe are fit for the completion
that lulls: lovers resist change   praise it. . .

City Service

in the very best lie

        you're thinking,

                they're together!

this is how some people must hurt themselves, through faulty allegiance.

anticipatory conjecture

to divide and spread

        a normal

            devotion to pain. . .

some people must hurt themselves more: thinking too much

               when thinking is doubting.

doubting myself and one conscious principle,

that is, the loss of myself

in a city of flagrant gain.

I walk between.

then stare-standing.

friends and enemies hold an overstated illusion of each other

they run through rain to catch elusive innocence

they shiver behind a devious dark

and once dancing

I angle between   they're process and they're pause.

It will take shape   this life of mine
I offer the pieces
          and when they are taken
I gather to them
– that's why I'll be in the future forever.

But the contrasts of daily life and theatre
eliminate all simple descriptions:
                              bums are asking for too little
          while well-ordered astronauts shape an inelegant earth,
                    thin women with eatable and plump fruit
     and friendly men with uninterested greyhounds pass simultaneously,
as a passive city compiles
                              its aggressive smells;
I can not yet congratulate myself for spending
an ordinary day
          watching many find for each other
                    the injury that is warmth.
we won't be found and that's that.
I wash my hands
and travel a new street.

                    As hardness wears dull
                         the hard dullness wears
me strict. . .

over the first mark I see severed buildings

cripple stone

crunched brick ended,   breaking off

in arteries of steel,

girder veins seared off

by building fire,

lit molding

corpuscles of plaster

layers of bone   going up,

cells of nails

truncated arm to reach

hopes in stone,

protein   the builders go growing

up an unfinished thrill,

which work unbuilt

completes the stone to the sky

defines the remaining work of the city.

streets rough a raw on my skin   thick slabs of exterior peel off

I'm blood on the shot

as skin does not hold

through this while of red

in a city I'm exposed by underdevelopment

and can alone feel myself

disappear

in renown and underpublicized silence.

What contradictions

between people and structure

      produce a conflict

               of grand subtlety and no mercy!!

stone bubbles

        popping

buckles a gorge

by riot   teeth roll on

      a little talk

      subway whispers and

A Roar,   I'm alone,

. . .from the very long division of the city

         we divide ourselves into separation.

the reason that seeks

    I have absorbed

         to exaggerate. . .

to twist my turn on words again

and understate

      and be short and cold. . .

to overstate

      and when to dance, over dance

        music that imitates the poor.

        Oh distract us

from the persistent truth of that observable rule:

Which is,

We dare not

           reveal the full impulse   FORMing

              an urban and foreign soul.

Rather, Oh let us remain sure

that we collect unholy experiences

in an unholy place for lessons

clustered along a delicate process

leading to absolute victory. . .

Child Of Mercy

Then there was one severely deformed child

Posed (as grimly exposed in a lobby)

With an angular face, roughshod, unordered

In many errant parts as though God,

The Self, had flung a vagrant whim that way –

Flesh so heavy that a lower eye rim

Rolled down, a maddened maul racing red

To the place we dangle before all.

Once rewound, songs and passersby assume
Good looks and health even abound.

~

There's a story.
This is a story about the story.
The story has a protagonist, jokester,
one or two stand-ins,
and foreground and background,
and somebody gets hurt,
and another gets laid.
At the end, love doesn't conquer all,
but crime and redemption
were inevitable.
There's just one story,
repeated anew.

My Boy At Shiloh

*(our visit to Hardin County four
generations after the battle of 1862)*

A light flickers, and down into the boy
A photo darkens and casts a shade
On a May field in Tennessee.

For into sunken fables a diluvial echo
Takes the boy, hardly safe on print
Against a stone fence at Shiloh.

It wasn't for uniforms or famous killings
That conceit rang so loudly, but rather
One memory he couldn't own.

"I just wish to plot a crime I didn't see,"
As he stood on legends plowing deep,
The dead keeping secret the story.

"My family broken by it, a town pinched."
But he'll do better, for a survivor puts
Distance between bouts of pain.

Still, I fear, 'til he sees dead flesh mulch
Or his dank grip upon a dread shiv,
The shade gladly stays his own.

Darkness

What light do you crave on this tired earth?
Or do you come from darkness deeper in yourself? And hunchbacked
and shackled, drag darkness to the living? Do you tear
out someone else's darkness to hold it over them as a
hammer? Do you? Do you look for all that's hidden
or shy because, in your own dark mind, all that's hidden from you
becomes your own terror?

Do I see you search out a stranger
for the night? But Oh! All the living is a stranger to
you. Hear the steps in the park behind you? Notice a
madman watching? What of your home – black draperies and cold tile?
And how's your wife, stiff and afraid of your loud stares?
And your children? Or do you have children? Strange to see you there,
proud and acting alone –

your children shaking like leaves. Yes we
know your darkness is your own weak mind. But what of light? Oh
yes, you have light also, hidden in your shirt pocket
to work as a heart. You short-circuit the human race with a
bit of knowledge in a factory of darkness.
We know who came your way with a small thrill of fancy; now moths
are eating in her eyes –

she doesn't even care, she doesn't
even blow them away. What do you say? Darkness is best?
We have to know darkness before light? Does the night
warm me? Do cold invisible hands love me? Does darkness glow
in any lover's excited face? Oh light is
what I enjoy! We knew light absolutely first, and we will
grow and grow more and more

violent and impatient to be
re-taught in a clumsy night to follow darkness into
light. Yes we know freedom's light can also lead us to
darkness. Yes we know darkness is even older than sin and
at least twice as old as light. But we have only recently come,
so do not tell us about darkness, we can't understand.
Night will spread out with flames

and be just like day, light more real than darkness.
Old men will be glad to say it had to happen this way,
as we say to our children, "Do not destroy this light
or its freedom, nor scare freedom away by demanding too much
from it, for freedom can also be darkness when it becomes chaos.
Watch out for those who control but don't love and those
who would steal your light to feed their darkness."

Fear Of Flying

We're downtown on September 11th,
Minding our business, tending fate.
There's one moment,
Early in advance of the rest,
When birds don't sing being in flight,
When they wend alongside many a parched cornice;
No, they never sing without a grip.
(*And we want to be with God.*)

Around the corner, across from St. Paul's Chapel,
People take on air –
Some leap, while most degrade into vapor
In one giant cough, dropping headlong
Through flames or debris, never landing.
(*God, save them and us.*)

. . .Wait, we'd aerate effect to lighten the torque;
Balloons, yes, balloons
And footballs, kites, all
Fly so high a loose languor
As if ordained aloft in undiminishable space, retiring
Into well-stretched and elevated hands.
(*God meant for rare things to happen,*
But not for a man with a butcher knife
To cut an airborne tether.)

By hell's unchoked retch,
A gas-blackened plume heatedly swells
A swatch of cellophane heavenward, higher still.

How does it happen some things
Rise air-tucked without ties,
Staves, or other fast catch-mes? Atop
An attenuating breath,
The swath should land but when?

(". . .Wisdom comes once
We've taken place.")

So there.
Flying is good for business, we're told,
But is it good for us?

The Other

I whispered heresy:
Be small and thankful
you're not popular,
for you don't need
      to recall sales
nor nod at a vendor
nor pretend
      not to see.

They look lost there
      with scrupulous grins
and an entourage
      extruding faith
and contrast.

Sure you envy their teeth
but not the gross claims
they must eat for breakfast.

Yet
once popular,
you'd hardly be
unpopular soon.

Quatrains

~

You must always be ready to adjust:
People lose office, automobiles start to rust.
As things fall apart and become unrated,
So loss is normalcy gone unabated.

~

Listen, my sweet,
So you will hear:
A worthwhile feat
Is knowing to fear.

~

What should they be like,
The ones we can't dislike?
You know, those who carry a big stick
And contribute to some political prick.

~

Catch a falling star
And put him in your pocket.
He's found at the bar,
Drinking in thoughts of a rocket.

~

She says to keep your hands above your waist,
You naughty boy, and learn to control your haste;
But you are no young boy any longer
With your flair for rite to do wronger.

~

When we are already dense and old,
Steadfastly at rest, collecting mold,
We will, instead, for a more private concern,
Recall these hours, which we will yet relearn.

~

I used to say a lot
Before smarts I got.
Now I say a lot less
And get into less mess.

~

Let me know you,
But not too well.
Keep both of us true,
Give nothing to tell.

~

So you like the contours of time,
Counting seconds and minutes in rhyme.
To grow older, you say, means a loss of power,
For you expect less from each passing hour.

~

Friends should not be tampered with
But aged the way of a very good fifth.
They should be held close,
Yet not in a great big dose.

~

I missed the opportunity to exploit.
That's either bad or ethically adroit.
If I could be so sure,
I'd say I'm also pure.

~

Expect the worst,
And you'll be first.
Expect the best,
You'll be put to rest.

~

Why should we exaggerate?
Otherwise, we simply don't rate.
It takes something special to be heard,
So lie a bit to find the right word.

~

To start the day, we think about food.
To end it, a snack for a change in mood.
And in between, we curse work until a meal.
It's a way of searching for the original deal.

~

I've tried it all:
Fun, wine and gall.
So leave me alone
And let me moan.

~

It's the missing
And the kissing
She can only think about
Once she's left lover and lout.

~

Send my regrets to the egrets,
My apologies to the manatees;
For the urge was great and my bladder grew,
So I took a piss in the ocean blue.

~

Is it man as horse
That I become?
Swayback, on a dirt course,
Going dumb. . .

~

Go ahead, get mad at me, you dope;
Why shouldn't I feel the sting of an intimate rope?
But let me tell you one thing, you jerk –
Anger to show you care simply doesn't work.

~

Where are they now, one asks,
Uncles of the broken masks?
Under cover of lucent night,
They go naked to be contrite.

~

How much do I have left?
That's what I keep asking myself,
As I go about meeting deadlines,
Collecting tickets, paying fines.

~

Once a warm voice came
Making the whole lame,
As pieces of a hard sale broke apart
To splinter roughly through the heart.

~

We divide our lives into two frames:
The first forty years and future games.
We're much better at planning the first,
Though the second's meant to quench our thirst.

~

What a relief! The winds of war are over.
The howls of midnight leave without a slur.
The job is over, and I'll be normal again.
But first, a little wine and maybe a little sin.

~

One last hurrah before the lights go down,
Something to scare the pants off a town.
A little spice is always nice,
Even if it consists of liquor and dice.

~

You are growing up, my daughter, at an alarming rate,
And your mental and physical portions have a traded state;
But what I have long thought proves much harder to take –
The size of change alters all things in its wake.

~

Some say they're poets
But simply have no ear;
Others, who say they're not,
Quite write like Will Shakespeare.

~

When boring, we're not to be forgiven,
Even if it were for humor we were driven.
That glazed look, my God, that punishing disregard;
It's wholly my fault, or it wouldn't be so hard.

~

You enjoy yourself a little more,
As years burn down the sharp edges –
Round, smooth, so withdrawn to ignore
And walking further from the ledges.

~

While an older allegory throughout,
Our practice put our ingenuity to rout;
And we could not bear to stop,
Even to let a writing hand drop.

~

Let others speak,
You won't be meek.
You'll stay put
And save a foot.

~

It takes us a very long time to believe
That enjoyment can be a long-term reprieve;
We spend much of our hard, younger years
Trying to screw up our natural gears.

~

The pressures of the job drained away the abundance of time,
And everything was sacrificed for the job's consuming crime.
Now that the effort's over, what a relief;
And I still have time to turn a new leaf.

~

It's rather disgusting, I've come to believe,
How we take one last attempt to achieve.
There's simply no way to begin a retreat,
Unless we admit we're incessantly incomplete.

~

Some want money.
Some just excitement.
Some want to be.
But you and I just went.

~

Great stories have simple plots,
Good and evil, accurate slots;
They stay out of ditches
And stay clear of glitches.

~

Liquor makes the head swirl around;
Three sips, and numerous triumphs abound.
One becomes the last wise king of the hill,
Who incidentally re-stoked the still.

~

Go against the grain,
You'll honor the pain.
Step across a fine line
And enjoy the dark wine.

~

Do not stop short,
Or choose to thwart;
Something has to have length
If it plans to have strength.

~

Do things halfway,
Don't forget to play;
For completion imitates death,
And conclusions stop a breath.

~

Who tries to broker hell
Has something special to sell.
Who tries to broker hell
Has a miserable fact to quell.

~

One has to be late now and then
Just to show that one is needed.
But when you arrive, don't ever grin:
People act on ways they're treated.

~

The speed calms down,
The muscles groan,
My bones turn brown,
My limbs to stone.

~

We cope with the dark side,
The fire that has lied.
We agree to compromise
And stay a smaller size.

~

I grew up with a TV
And didn't know any better.
Now I play "dot-com" and "e,"
And I'm safer a netter.

~

God just wants me to mature,
Not to be beautiful or pure.
So God chose to use events
For my questions to make sense.

~

Who's beyond the law?
One without flaw?
One who alone will know
Where the law can not go.

~

Don't be so profound,
You're not the last one found.
To talk ever so serious
Makes one ever so delirious.

~

As a rule, brains prevail,
Hold seminars and rail.
One thing remains some unclear:
Why we don't like them too near.

~

To lure the light,
Don't just sigh.
Auden was right:
Laugh and die.

~

Shorts are for fun:
No long-winded run,
No pompous strut
Or wide butt.

~

Who is satisfied?
The one ratified
Or the one fortified?
No, the one implied.

Haiku

~

He found a language
He could employ to explore
The voice within him.

~

Trying too hard, Bud,
Is walking backwards slowly
In a fast footrace.

~

Starlets, muscles-galore, stud
Share a common shtick:
Bad bods are a dud.

~

Chatter, chatter, the
Trio hadn't a noun on
Quiet audio.

~

Money is the root
Of all evil but is the
Subject of most verbs.

~

It's the brute and bland
TV selling sky
With a piece or two in hand.

~

Stones shall cry out faith,
But there's none if I know the
Ultimate outcome.

~

One need not be a flake
Nor nibbler of the opaque
To savor Pope.

~

A hand to wield and
A mind to thwart, a will to tear
A house apart.

~

He heard a small voice
If he thought small, a loud one
If he changed at all.

~

Faulkner a few rednecks
And Poe ravens, but
Stevens had insurance.

~

Much verse is being
Written, not from the heart, but
From the pancreas.

~

To revise is to
Argue – excess to access
And more into less.

~

To be satisfied
In our little cells of twilight
Is heroic.

Chapbooks By J. Chester Johnson

Oh America & January 12th, 1967

Shorts: For Fun, Not For Instruction

It's A Long Way Home / An American Sequence

Shorts: On Reaching Forty

Family Ties, Internecine Interregnum!

For Conduct and Innocents

The Professional Curiosity Of A Martyr

Exile / Martin

Freda's Appetite

Lazarus, Come Forth and Plain Bob (Unbehaved)